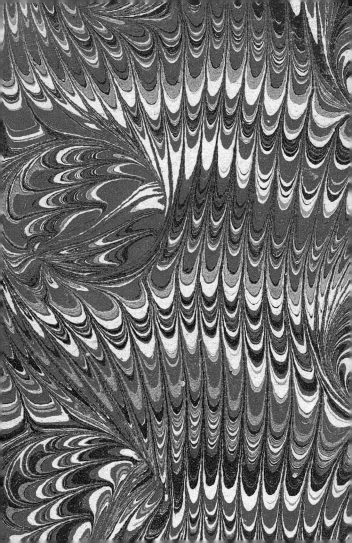

THE
WISDOM
OF

G. K.
Chesterton

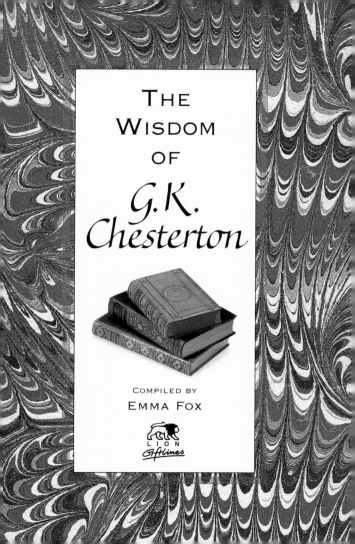

COMPILED BY
EMMA FOX

LION
Giftlines

This edition copyright © 1997 Lion Publishing

Published by
Lion Publishing plc
Sandy Lane West, Oxford, England
ISBN 0 7459 3931 7

First edition 1997
10 9 8 7 6 5 4 3 2 1 0

A catalogue record for this book is available
from the British Library

Printed and bound in Singapore

Series editor: Meryl Doney
Project editor: Angela Handley
Jacket designer: Jonathan Roberts
Cover and first page illustration: David Axtell

Contents

G.K. Chesterton is probably best-known today for his Father Brown detective stories, but in his lifetime he was celebrated as a writer and speaker, producing not only short stories but biography, poetry, history, essays, novels, reviews, political manifestos and a play.

He was perhaps at his best – and happiest – when engaged in intellectual battle. He had long-running and famous public controversies with leading atheists such as H.G. Wells and George Bernard Shaw but his favourite target was the unquestioned tenets of fashionable opinion. The questions he tackled are still relevant: genetic engineering, birth-control, the position of women, the failures of capitalism, and the secularization of Christianity.

He was a man with many intellectual opponents but, famously, no enemies: both Wells and Shaw became good friends. His breadth of appeal continues. The sceptic Martin Gardner says of Chesterton's stories, 'the metaphysical messages are worth pondering regardless of your beliefs, even if you are an atheist' and Terry Pratchett dedicates his novel *Good Omens* to Chesterton, 'a man who knew what was going on.'

Chesterton's religious writing can be extremely persuasive. C.S. Lewis' famous conversion from atheism came on the heels of reading *The Everlasting Man*. Likewise, readers of the Father Brown detective stories may well emerge to find themselves (like me, and many before me) being received into the Church. Alec Guinness encountered the same phenomenon after merely portraying Brown on screen. Indeed, Father Brown had a similar effect on Chesterton himself. He was neither a Christian nor a Catholic when he started the series: as one critic puts it – 'it took Father Brown eleven years to convert his creator.'

Such openness to the full consequences of his own thought is surely part of the secret of Chesterton's persuasiveness: he is intellectually fearless. No reader can argue with him more vigorously than he already has with himself. Like his beloved Aquinas, his whole argument begins: 'Is there a God? Apparently not.' His strongly held beliefs come as a result of his thoroughly practical intellectual, political and ethical enquiries. As he explains in Extract 28 he first looks around and encounters 'a hole in the world' and only then does he discover 'the spike of dogma' that fits it exactly.

Born in London in l874, Chesterton soon launched himself on a lifetime's career in journalism. His first novel, *The Napoleon of Notting Hill* was followed in l908 by what many consider to be his best novel, *The Man Who Was Thursday*. His output continued prolifically on all fronts: his secretary recalls his ability to dictate one article while writing another. He also wrote hugely successful book-length studies of, amongst others, Browning, Dickens, St Francis of Assisi and St Thomas Aquinas. The volume on Browning is distinguished, as Chesterton himself later noticed, by containing only two dates – both of them wrong. His biographies were, nevertheless, uniquely successful in capturing the essence of their subjects. The final appearance of *Aquinas* sparked critical awareness that Chesterton's lively wit and jaunty style belied the considerable intellect beneath. The critics declared it to be 'the best book ever written on St Thomas. Nothing short of genius can account for such an achievement.'

In summarizing his varied achievements, it is easy to loose sight of one overriding fact about Chesterton the writer. He is very funny. He tells funny stories – don't miss the episode of the Oswego biscuit in *Autobiography*. And he is unfailingly witty. P.J. Kavanagh talks of 'the continual pleasure to be derived (merely) from Chesterton's tone'. This sustained and inherent humour springs from his two most constant delights. The first of these is the universe itself – his astonishment, humility and gratitude over the wild fact that the universe exists and that somehow we can participate in its story. The second is his delight in small things. Only Chesterton could write an essay – one of his best – on *Running After One's Hat*; or again, he founds the entire theological argument in his *Autobiography* on the mere act of looking at a dandelion. This lightness of touch, however, is not based on a simplistic optimism. Chesterton is only too aware of the presence and power of evil. He says 'I am not proud of knowing the Devil.' Yet he has wrestled to the intellectual and spiritual conclusion that there is something – and Someone – far greater. The humour he is able to embody and express is thus truly part of the joy of God's good creation.

Chesterton's work suffered a brief fall from fashion in the middle of the century but today his popularity continues to grow. The Ignatius Press in New York has begun the daunting task of re-publishing his complete works. There is also a popular movement in favour of his canonization. I believe Chesterton would have approached this eventuality with the awe and humility which so monumental a question deserves – then he would have laughed. He spent his life, after all, in discovering the joy, and the laughter, that lies at the very heart of the ultimate solemnity of God.

EMMA FOX

Beginnings

ONE SEES GREAT
THINGS FROM THE
VALLEY, ONLY SMALL
THINGS FROM
THE PEAK.

FROM
*THE INNOCENCE OF
FATHER BROWN*

THOUGHT ITSELF

At a very early age I had thought my way back to thought itself. It is a very dreadful thing to do; for it may lead to thinking that there is nothing but thought... While dull atheists came and explained to me that there was nothing but matter, I listened with a sort of calm horror of detachment, suspecting that there was nothing but mind. I have always felt that there was something thin and third-rate about materialists and materialism ever since. The atheist told me so pompously that he did not believe there was any God; and there were moments when I did not even believe there was any atheist.

FROM *AUTOBIOGRAPHY*

St Thomas Aquinas practically begins his whole argument by saying, 'Is there a God? Apparently not.'

FROM *AUTOBIOGRAPHY*

WITH NEW EYES

I spoke of the strange daylight [of childhood], which was something more than the light of common day, that still seems in my memory to shine on those steep roads down from Campden Hill, from which one could see the Crystal Palace from afar. Well, when a Catholic comes from Confession, he does truly, by definition, step out again into that dawn of his own beginning and look with new eyes across the world to a Crystal Palace that is really of crystal. He believes that in that dim corner, and in that brief ritual, God has really re-made him in his own image. He is now a new experiment of the Creator. He is as much a new experiment as he was when he was really only five years old. He stands, as I said, in the white light at the worthy beginning of the life of a man. The accumulations of time can no longer terrify. He may be grey and gouty; but he is only five minutes old.

FROM *AUTOBIOGRAPHY*

3

SIMPLICITY

So very simple is the road,
That we may stray from it.

FROM *COLLECTED POEMS*

St Francis of Assisi never forgot to take pleasure in a bird as it flashed past him, or a drop of water as it fell from his finger: he was, perhaps, the happiest of the sons of men. Yet this man undoubtedly founded his whole polity on the negation of what we think the most imperious necessities, in his three vows of poverty, chastity, and obedience.

ESSAY IN *THE SPEAKER*

HUMILITY

The secret of life lies in laughter and humility.

FROM *HERETICS*

When fishes flew and forests walked
And figs grew upon thorn,
Some moment when the moon was blood
Then surely I was born.

With monstrous head and sickening cry
And ears like errant wings,
The devil's walking parody
On all four-footed things.

The tattered outlaw of the earth,
Of ancient crooked will;
Starve, scourge, deride me: I am dumb,
I keep my secret still.

Fools! For I also had my hour;
One far fierce hour and sweet:
There was a shout about my ears,
And palms before my feet.

'THE DONKEY' FROM *COLLECTED POEMS*

FAITH

[*Father Brown has discovered and then released a man who stole the priceless table settings at a dinner attended by an exclusive and very wealthy club – The Twelve True Fishermen. Father Brown returns the stolen goods.*]

Father Brown got to his feet, putting his hands behind him. 'Odd, isn't it,' he said, 'that a thief and a vagabond should repent, when so many who are rich and secure remain hard and frivolous, and without fruit for God or man? But there, if you will excuse me, you trespass a little upon my province. If you doubt the penitence as a practical fact, there are your knives and forks. You are The Twelve True Fishers, and there are all your silver fish. But he has made me a fisher of men.'

'Did you catch this man?' asked the colonel, frowning.

Father Brown looked him full in his frowning face. 'Yes,' he said, 'I caught him, with an unseen hook and an invisible line which is long enough to let him wander to the ends of the world, and still to bring him back with a twitch upon the thread.'

FROM *THE INNOCENCE OF FATHER BROWN*

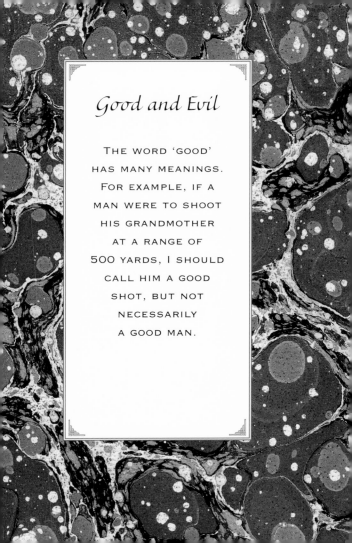

Good and Evil

THE WORD 'GOOD'
HAS MANY MEANINGS.
FOR EXAMPLE, IF A
MAN WERE TO SHOOT
HIS GRANDMOTHER
AT A RANGE OF
500 YARDS, I SHOULD
CALL HIM A GOOD
SHOT, BUT NOT
NECESSARILY
A GOOD MAN.

GOOD INTENTIONS

That 'God looked on all things and saw that they were good' contains a subtlety which the popular pessimist cannot follow; or is too hasty to notice. It is the thesis that there are no bad things but only bad thoughts; and especially bad intentions. Only Calvinists can really believe that the road to hell is paved with good intentions. That is exactly the one thing it cannot be paved with.

FROM *ST THOMAS AQUINAS*

SOMETHING FLAMING

Virtue is not the absence of vices or the avoidance of moral dangers; virtue is a vivid and separate thing, like pain or a particular smell. Mercy does not mean not being cruel or sparing people revenge or punishment; it means a plain and positive thing like the sun, which one has either seen or not seen. Chastity does not mean abstention from sexual wrong; it means something flaming, like Joan of Arc.

FROM *SELECTED ESSAYS*

THE WORLD STATE

Oh, how I love Humanity,
With love so pure and pringlish,
And how I hate the horrid French,
Who never will be English!

The International Idea,
The largest and the clearest,
Is welding all the nations now,
Except the one that's nearest.

This compromise has long been known,
This scheme of partial pardons,
In ethical societies
And small suburban gardens –

The villas and the chapels where
I learned with little labour,
The way to love my fellow-man
And hate my next-door neighbour.

FROM *A MOTLEY WISDOM*

THE CASE AGAINST CRIME

There is this about such evil, that it opens door after door in hell, and always into smaller and smaller chambers. This is the real case against crime, that a man does not become wilder and wilder, but only meaner and meaner.

FROM *THE INNOCENCE OF FATHER BROWN*

RUNNING WILD

[With the coming of Christianity] we must be much more angry with theft than before, and yet much kinder to thieves than before. There was room for wrath and love to run wild. And the more I considered Christianity, the more I found that while it had established a rule and order, the chief aim of that order was to give room for good things to run wild.

FROM *ORTHODOXY*

The Surprising Universe

IS DITCHWATER DULL?
NATURALISTS WITH
MICROSCOPES HAVE
TOLD ME THAT IT TEEMS
WITH QUIET FUN.

FROM *THE SPICE OF LIFE*

PUDDLES AND TURKEYS

What... is a puddle? A puddle repeats infinity, and is full of light; nevertheless, if analysed objectively, a puddle is a piece of dirty water spread very thin on mud.

FROM *MANALIVE*

A turkey is more occult and awful than all the angels and archangels. In so far as God has partly revealed to us an angelic world, he has partly told us what an angel means. But God has never told us what a turkey means. And if you go and stare at a live turkey for an hour or two, you will find by the end of it that the enigma has rather increased than diminished.

FROM *ALL THINGS CONSIDERED*

A FRAME OF MIND

Melancholy should be an innocent interlude, a tender and fugitive frame of mind; praise should be the permanent pulsation of the soul.

FROM *ORTHODOXY*

UPROARIOUS LABOUR

Pessimism is at best an emotional half-holiday; joy is the uproarious labour by which all things live.

FROM *ORTHODOXY*

A BALLADE OF SUICIDE

The gallows in my garden, people say,
    Is new and neat and adequately tall.
I tie the noose on in a knowing way
    As one that knots his necktie for a ball;
But just as all the neighbours – on the wall –
Are drawing a long breath to shout 'Hurray!'
The strangest whim has seized me… After all
    I think I will not hang myself to-day.

To-morrow is the time I get my pay –
    My uncle's sword is hanging in the hall –
I see a little cloud all pink and grey –
    Perhaps the Rector's mother will *not* call –
I fancy that I heard from Mr Gall
That mushrooms could be cooked another way –
    I never read the works of Juvenal –
    I think I will not hang myself to-day.

…And through thick woods one finds
            a stream astray,
So secret that the very sky seems small –
    I think I will not hang myself to-day.

FROM *COLLECTED POEMS*

EARTH'S ARITHMETIC

I cannot count the pebbles in the brook.
Well hath he spoken: 'Swear not by thy head,
Thou knowest not the hairs,' though he, we read,
Writes that wild number in his own strange book.

I cannot count the sands or search the seas,
Death cometh, and I leave so much untrod.
Grant my immortal aureole, O my God,
And I will name the leaves upon the trees.

In heaven I shall stand on gold and glass,
Still brooding earth's arithmetic to spell;
Or see the fading of the fires of hell
Ere I have thanked my God for all the grass.

'ETERNITIES' FROM *POEMS FOR ALL PURPOSES*

Playful as a Child

THE TRUE OBJECT
OF ALL HUMAN LIFE
IS PLAY. EARTH IS
A TASK GARDEN;
HEAVEN IS A
PLAYGROUND.

FROM *A MOTLEY WISDOM*

Mr Chesterton

A small guest at a children's party in Beaconsfield was asked when he got home whether Mr Chesterton had been very clever. 'I don't know about clever,' was the reply, 'but you should see him catch buns in his mouf.'

RONALD KNOX ON G.K. CHESTERTON

I f a thing is worth doing, it is worth doing badly.

FROM *WHAT IS WRONG WITH THE WORLD*

RUNNING AFTER ONE'S HAT

[Running after one's hat when the wind blows it off] certainly is comic; but man is a very comic creature, and most of the things he does are comic – eating for instance. And the most comic things of all are exactly the things that are most worth doing – such as making love... When last I saw an old gentleman running after his hat in Hyde Park, I told him that a heart so benevolent as his ought to be filled with peace and thanks at the thought of how much unaffected pleasure his every gesture and bodily attitude were at that moment giving to the crowd...

FROM *SELECTED ESSAYS*

The repetition in Nature seemed sometimes to be an excited repetition... The grass seemed signalling to me with all its fingers at once; the crowded stars seemed bent upon being understood... The recurrences of the universe rose to the maddening rhythm of an incantation, and I began to see an idea... Because children have abounding vitality, because they are in spirit fierce and free, therefore they want things repeated and unchanged. They always say, 'do it again'; and the grown-up person does it again until he is nearly dead. For grown-up people are not strong enough to exult in monotony. It is possible that God says every morning, 'Do it again' to the sun; and every evening, 'Do it again' to the moon... It may be that he has the eternal appetite of infancy; for we have sinned and grown old, and our Father is younger than we.

FROM *ORTHODOXY*

WINE AND WATER

Old Noah he had an ostrich farm and fowls
on the largest scale,
He ate his egg with a ladle in an egg-cup
big as a pail,
And the soup he took was Elephant Soup
and the fish he took was Whale,
But they all were small to the cellar he took
when he set out to sail,
And Noah he often said to his wife
when he sat down to dine,
'I don't care where the water goes
if it doesn't get into the wine.'

FROM *COLLECTED POEMS*

DRAWING ON THE CEILING

L ying in bed would be an altogether perfect and supreme experience if only one had a coloured pencil long enough to draw on the ceiling. This, however, is not generally a part of the domestic apparatus on the premises. I think myself that the thing might be managed with several pails of Aspinall and a broom. Only if one worked in a really sweeping and masterly way, and laid on the colour in great washes, it might drip down again on one's face in floods of rich and mingled colour like some strange fairy rain; and that would have its disadvantages...

FROM *SELECTED ESSAYS*

Contending for the Truth

I BELIEVE IN GETTING
INTO HOT WATER.
I THINK IT KEEPS
YOU CLEAN.

PHILOSOPHIES

A new philosophy generally means in practice the praise of some old vice.

FROM *ALL THINGS CONSIDERED*

Of nearly all other philosophies it is strictly true that their followers work in spite of them… No materialist who thinks his mind was made up for him, by mud and blood and heredity, has any hesitation in making up his mind. No sceptic who believes that truth is subjective has any hesitation about treating it as objective.

FROM *ST THOMAS AQUINAS*

[In abandoning Christianity] we cannot pretend to be abandoning the morality of the past for one more suited to the present. It is certainly not the morality of another age, but it might be of another world… Whatever else is true, it is emphatically not true that the ideas of Jesus of Nazareth were suitable to his time, but are no longer suitable to our time. Exactly how suitable they were to his time is perhaps suggested in the end of his story.

FROM *THE EVERLASTING MAN*

The Christian ideal has not been tried and found wanting. It has been found difficult; and left untried.

FROM *WHAT IS WRONG WITH THE WORLD*

REASONABLE DOGMA

I am proud of being fettered by antiquated dogmas and enslaved by dead creeds (as my journalistic friends repeat with so much pertinacity), for I know very well that it is the heretical creeds that are dead and that it is only the reasonable dogma that lives long enough to be called antiquated.

FROM *AUTOBIOGRAPHY*

THE WORLD IS ROUND

Don't say 'There is no true creed; for each creed believes itself right and the other wrong.' Diversity does show that most of the views must be wrong. It does not by the faintest logic show that they all must be wrong... I believe (merely upon authority) that the world is round. That there may be tribes who believe it to be triangular or oblong does not alter the fact that it is certainly some shape, and therefore not any other shape. Therefore I repeat, with the wail of imprecation, don't say that the variety of creeds prevents you from accepting any creed. It is an unintelligent remark.

FROM AN ESSAY IN *THE DAILY NEWS*

THE SUNRISE OF WONDER

The object of the artistic and spiritual life was to dig for this submerged sunrise of wonder; so that a man sitting in a chair might suddenly understand that he was actually alive, and be happy.

FROM *AUTOBIOGRAPHY*

Going Home

YOU NEVER
LAUGHED IN
ALL YOUR LIFE
AS I SHALL
LAUGH IN
DEATH.

FROM *WISDOM AND
INNOCENCE:
A LIFE OF G.K. CHESTERTON*

Yet by God's death the stars shall stand
And the small apples grow.

FROM *POEMS FOR ALL PURPOSES*

Christianity has died many times and risen again; for it had a god who knew the way out of the grave.

FROM *THE EVERLASTING MAN*

GOLD LEAVES

Lo! I am come to autumn,
When all the leaves are gold;
Grey hairs and golden leaves cry out
The year and I are old.

In youth I sought the prince of men,
Captain in cosmic wars,
Our Titan, even the weeds would show
Defiant, to the stars.

But now a great thing in the street
Seems any human nod,
Where shift in strange democracy
The million masks of God.

In youth I sought the golden flower
Hidden in wood or wold,
But I am come to autumn,
When all the leaves are gold.

FROM *COLLECTED POEMS*

A HOLE IN THE WORLD

I had found [a] hole in the world; the fact that one must somehow find a way of loving the world without trusting it; [then] I found… Christian theology [and] the dogmatic insistence that God was personal, and had made a world separate from himself. The spike of dogma fitted exactly into the hole in the world… I was right when I felt that roses were red by some sort of choice: it was the divine choice… The fancy that the cosmos was not vast and void, but small and cosy, had a fulfilled significance now, for anything that is a work of art must be small in the sight of the artist; to God the stars might be only small and dear, like diamonds… The modern philosopher had told me again and again that I was in the right place, and I had still felt depressed even in acquiescence. But I had heard that I was in the *wrong* place, and my soul sang for joy, like a bird in spring. The knowledge found out and illuminated forgotten chambers in the dark house of infancy. I knew now why grass had always seemed to me as queer as the green beard of a giant, and why I could feel homesick at home.

FROM *ORTHODOXY*

IN PATRIA

[*Chesterton often quoted the two-word definition of heaven, and it is included in the lines from Aquinas that are carved upon Chesterton's gravestone.*]

'*In patria*' – it tells you everything: 'our native land'.

FROM MAISIE WARD, *RETURN TO CHESTERTON*

THE ROLLING ENGLISH ROAD

For there is good news yet to hear
and fine things to be seen,
Before we go to Paradise
by way of Kensal Green.

FROM *POEMS FOR ALL PURPOSES*

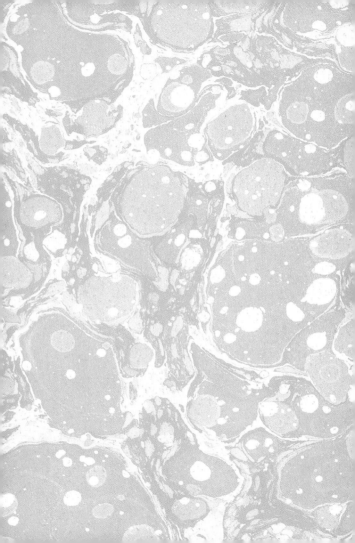

TEXT ACKNOWLEDGMENTS

Extracts from *Heretics*, *Return to Chesterton*, *G.K. Chesterton: A Half-Century of Views* (edited by D.J. Conlon; G.K. Chesterton quotation only), an essay in *The Daily News*, *All Things Considered*, *Manalive*, *Selected Essays* ('A Piece of Chalk', 'On Running After One's Hat', On Lying in a Bed'), *The Spice of Life*, *St Thomas Aquinas*, *Collected Poems* ('The Wise Men', 'The Donkey' (entire poem), 'A Ballad of Suicide', 'Wine and Water', 'Gold Leaves' (entire poem)), *The Speaker*, *Poems for All Purposes: The Selected Poems of G.K. Chesterton* (edited by Stephen Medcalf) ('Eternities' (entire poem), 'The Ballad of the White Horse', 'The Rolling English Road'), *Autobiography* (edited by Antony Tyler), *Orthodoxy*, *What is Wrong with the World*, *The Everlasting Man* and *The Innocence of Father Brown* by G.K. Chesterton, reproduced by permission of A.P. Watt Ltd on behalf of the Royal Literary Fund.

Extracts from *A Motley Wisdom: The Best of G.K. Chesterton* by G.K. Chesterton (edited by Nigel Forde). Copyright © 1995 Nigel Forde. Reproduced by permission of Hodder and Stoughton Limited.

Extract from *Wisdom and Innocence: A Life of G.K. Chesterton* by Joseph Pearce. Copyright © Joseph Pearce, 1996. Reproduced by permission of Hodder and Stoughton Limited.